Darkest

DEV BHATTACHARYYA

DevbInc

Published by Devb Inc. https://www.devb.com

ISBN: 0-9978887-0-9
ISBN-13: 978-0-9978887-0-6

DEDICATION

To the Lord

He who knows the Lord within
For him church-doors are always open

*

Mithoo
Departed Sha and Kay

CONTENTS

FUTILE NEGOTIATION

Intense is the dark, slow is his flight
Clouds pause. With vigor dances the rain
But the dark? Day is it or night?
Likely night; the ruddy swan is his own self again

No one spoke a word. D'thor, weary and tired, glanced at the darkened sky as he stepped down the palace stairs and alighted his chariot. Several eyes followed his departure, but most stood in silence, busy battling their thoughts, busy piecing the outcome of the meeting. Ninety long years, D'thor had sought peace; peace among the chieftains, among the monarchs and the emperors.

For a moment, his mind drifted to his son and queen in the city of Flence; then he cast the thoughts aside and threw a departing glance at the empty palace steps. The midday overcast sun cast an indistinct shadow on the landing, an undisguised omen that all talks of peace were now futile. Drake, his trusted charioteer had cautioned D'thor of the uselessness of the meeting. D'thor smiled back at the inquisitive face, the bland smile said it all - the meeting had not gone well. He looked again at the shadow on the landing; it pointed to the palace gates. He at once nodded to Drake. As the car turned into the narrow road that led to an exit, D'thor glanced at the occasional empty stalls constrained by the thicket. 'An empty palindrome, much like its king that yields nothing whichever way you twist it - left or the right', he mused. Just when the nimble car weaved past the stalls, D'thor gripped Drake's shoulder, nudging him to stop.

He sprang from the moving car and strode towards the man who stood selling the last of the garlands he had strewn in the early hours of the dawn. The seller had just one customer and D'thor picked a long garland from the wicker basket and tiptoed behind the tall, mustached, auburn gentleman. "Such pretty flowers grow only in Lakewood," D'thor spoke to the stranger, his eyes on the garland. "Flowers that suit the nymphs and goddesses. And, the men - of course."

D'thor knew at once every movement was being watched. Hidden eyes and scopes lay everywhere. Arsenio watching through the celestial scope related to King Daniel how D'thor halted at the palace gates. The king, at once, intrigued by this sudden meeting turned his attention to Arsenio's narrative.

"D'thor!" The stranger at the garland store exclaimed. "I knew you were in town. Ah! Only young D'thor would dare compare nymphs to goddesses. What can Diane's son do for the lord?"

"Novio, I had a hunch I would find you here. Young, I am no longer, Novio, I am catching up to your peers. Age is but an excuse for clarity. Or, its inverse." The grin was infectious. D'thor continued, "You may have heard the meeting did not go as expected. We concluded nothing. Not surprising, we all seized the moment with our disagreements." D'thor placed the garland across his arm. "But, I wanted to have a word with you before Drake steers me on our long journey home. No politics. Just a few incidents I had not shared with you earlier."

"I am honored, D'thor, but, I am not sure I understand." Novio searched into his eyes. "A merchant's son knows nothing of battles, weapons and politics anyway", Novio let the sarcasm trail. "Begin D'thor, on what you plan to share."

"We can drive on my chariot to where the narrow river turns blue again." D'thor nodded towards the fast-flowing stream. "It's a short ride and I promise to bring you back here." Novio looked again at the impassive face. The charm and twinkle in the hazel eyes bore no malice.

4

"I will soon be on my way, Novio. Away from Lakewood, for many days. You have nothing to lose, but to listen - one old man to another. And, I have the honor today to buy the remaining garland," D'thor handed a coin to the seller, put the garland around his neck and smiled at Novio.

"Accepted," Novio yielded, after a little hesitation. As he turned to instruct the merchant, D'thor walked to Drake and whispered to him, the new interim destination, then climbed the car, holding the intricate door for Novio. The whiff of jasmines and roses from the garlands filled the surrounding space. Novio's flush was unmistakable - the hard-tanned skin, matched the frown as the bleary sun stood at mid-point. The chariot jerked to life, though none spoke much while the three-steed car sped through the alluvial soil spread over concrete, scattering dirt and snapping soggy twigs.

As the car slowed down, D'thor held Novio's hand in his and spoke to him from the heart. "You sir, are the bravest among your people. Your generosity resonates far into the distant hills, you are an exemplar of excellence." He said. "But Novio, why do you endorse this evil war?"

Novio switched on his defenses. He turned his gaze away from D'thor to a large flock of dolphins gamboling in the deep river. "All my life, I have confronted contempt. People have ridiculed my low birth" Novio replied, moving his hand away as a deep anger surfaced on his brows. "Only Rodrigo gave me what no one will - his friendship. He never

5

failed in his support. Only two people ever gave me such unconditional love - my mother Diane and Rodrigo. My life, whatever it's worth - is for them."

"I commend your loyalty, Novio," for his incredible size, D'thor spoke in a gentle voice. "But I can assure you, the five-bejeweled princes and I did not spend our childhood on beds of roses. We all have our share of setbacks. Though I came to know you and the exiled princes at Jada's wedding, I know a few facts you don't. Such as your birth, and who your real mother is." D'thor stepped away from the car, nodding Novio to join him. In quick strides, he reached the slopes of the river bank. Carefully he bent and cupped a flower floating in the turgid waters. As he let the water drain through his fingers, he watched the fishes swim towards the disturbance.

"Know this, Novio," he spoke as his eyes trailed the dozen fishes that swarmed below in the shallow enclave. "Born you were of the Sun god. Your mother's a royal princess who was unwed when your birth took place. She is the mother of five other sons, brave and valorous as you." D'thor paused, "Son of Diane," he continued in an impassive voice, "many teachers tutored you on different subjects. And, you enquired of the wise, the accuracy of all known postulates. You learnt from the wise how to discern the eternal wisdom and laws. The old laws cite the example of Hans and Fester born to a maiden. Such children have for their father, the man who in due course marries the maid."

6

"Your birth, Novio, is no different." D'thor paused, "You are the legitimate son of the late king Aaron Sr. I invite you to his kingdom, so far denied to you. On one side you have the sons of Agata, the five princes and on the maternal side, you have my loyal kindred of Thorean-s." With a startled look, Novio mumbled something. His dry mouth and an intense pressure on his temples and knuckles drowned his speech. While his voice protested, D'thor looked at Novio with kind but impatient eyes, his hands gesturing Novio to not interrupt, but listen.

"Men revere you as a bull among them, Novio. Under your rule, you can prove to your people how much stronger this army and kingdom shall become. This day, let the announcement run as fast the speediest courier, O sire, that the five-bejeweled princes have an elder brother, a son of Agata, born before Aaron Jr. Let the five sons, their children born of Jada, and the invincible son of my half-sister Ema extoll you as their king. Other kings and princes along with the Thorean-s assembled in battle crease, supporting the five-princes' cause - let them embrace your feet. Let every king, queen and princess shower you in precious metal, gold and silver, and bathe you in the best of spring-water, while they anoint you with delicate herbs. I assure you; Jada will be yours." D'thor persisted. "Best of priests, Janek will preside over your coronation. All the five princes, their family priest, five children born of them, and I shall acclaim your ascending the throne, heralding a new era on this planet. O righteous Aaron descendent, your heir will run the kingdom under your instructions."

"Upon your coronation, Agata's son, mighty Hipolit, will hold the customary white parasol as you step into the open. Prince Alf shall steer your car furnished with a hundred tinkling bells. Jada's clan and the mighty car-warriors will be your convoy. Thorean army and I shall march in columns behind you. Enjoy the sovereignty of the planet, Novio. Even the empires extending to Acton in Northwest, Balerno, Everglades in Southwest and Arla in the East will step in with you. Proclaimed is such a triumph for you, Novio. It's everywhere. Surrounded by the five brothers, like the crowned moon by his many constellations, shall you rule the kingdom, O son of Agata. And, so shall you gladden your mother, Agata."

There was a momentary pause and the speech mellowed into a soft undertone. D'thor looked deep into Novio's eyes - an unmistakable honesty accompanied that look. "Allies shall rejoice, your enemies shall grieve. Let such a day mark a true reunion of you and your brothers. Six sons of Aaron Senior, together. Finally."

Novio's breathing streamed as short, tight gasps. If his heart beat any faster, it would burst. His eyes filled with tears; his face drained of color. Yet, fighting back the emotions, he stared in anger at D'thor. "Are you confirming the five exiled princes are my brothers, and their mother, Queen Agata - my mother?" he asked, his voice trembling with emotion. His face turned towards D'thor seeking an affirmation, the anger in his voice, rising, "Why are you telling me all this?"

8

Novio turned, his face recoiled in anger, "I don't doubt, D'thor, you mean well. Those words were spoken with no malice, but trust me, D'thor, I have died a thousand deaths just waiting to hear this." The revelation and the shock choked Novio's last words. Gently, D'thor held his shoulder. Novio searched again into his adversary's eyes, which were devoid of emotion.

"I knew from different sources Aaron Senior was my father." Novio blurted, "I figured, my mother, a maiden, carried me in her womb – a child of Sun god. Then, at Sun god's bidding, she abandoned me no sooner I stepped into this world."

"D'thor, I couldn't care less what happened ninety years before. My birth like anyone's - is in the past. Unreal, as it sounds, but it's true." Novio inhaled deep. The humid air soothed his bruised heart. "Legally, that makes me the son of my stepfather, Aaron Sr." He turned to D'thor, his anger on his nostrils. "But think of it, D'thor, that woman, Agata abandoned me with no thoughts of how I'd survive! She never even looked back, leaving me there to the mercy of wolves and canines. Not once did she look back!" His heavy voice boomed through the fog. "O D'thor, survive I did. And Salson, the merchant, held me in his loving arms, took me home. Diane, my mother, nurtured and cared for me. She attached no prerequisites to her love. No D'thor, no. These people are real. Not them." He gestured wildly at some imaginary people, gasping for air to regain his composure. "How can I? So well conversant in the laws, loyal to my duties, devoted to the scriptures, ever deprive a mother I have known for ninety plus years of her last rites?" Novio spoke, the voice drained of emotions.

"Salson raised me. That makes him a true father. O D'thor, Salson, like any father, left no stones unturned in caring for me in my early childhood. It is Salson, who gave me the name, Herkule. When I attained youth, he consented to my marriages. And now, D'thor, born of my beautiful wives, my sons and grandsons are my true heirs. Forsake them, D'thor? For this mere earth? Or, for heaps of gold? Never."

"I shall not desert Rodrigo, in whose empire I have reigned a king for the last thirteen years. You know well, in making me an ally, Rodrigo strengthens his ground forces. He becomes really prepared for any armed combat with the sons of Aaron." Novio stared at D'thor. "In such a battle, D'thor, I challenge Agata's son, Alf. Only one of us, Alf or I shall live to see another day."

"Tempt me not, D'thor, weak I may be, but to venture against Rodrigo? Never. And, D'thor, if I fail to engage Alf in a combat, I just spoke of; the end of our lives will be inglorious. D'thor, your narrative affirms my own findings." He retrieved a similar flower from the dusky waters. "I have no doubts, the five-bejeweled princes would, with no hesitation, abide to your propositions. But my faith and loyalty to Rodrigo stands firm."

10

Tossing the flower back into the river, Novio went on, "My battle with Alf is certain. But, I plead of you, D'thor, not to disclose this discourse of ours to anyone. I implore you. If Aaron ever gets to know of me as the firstborn son of Agata and he wins, he will not accept the coronation. And, if I win this mighty empire, I have only once choice – to turn it over to Rodrigo."

"I pray, Aaron becomes the new king. He has you for his guide and powerful forces - the Arla prince and other car-warriors. Then, you also have the Lambert ruler, Sabas, invincible Yoshi, Rufus brothers, the mighty car-warrior Santiago, and Emilio, son of Goro."

"Formidable is this assemblage, D'thor. I can imagine this new kingdom, endorsed by the kings of the earth, run by none other than Aaron. I foresee a great ceremony, a great sacrifice of arms – celebrated. The central theme in the ceremony is the slaughter of Rodrigo. And, you D'thor, as the head of the ceremony, oversee the operations of the sacrificial pyre. In this sacrifice, you even assume the office of administrator."

"Lucio presides as the first priest. The celestial bow appearing from nowhere churns the warriors' skills like a brisk ladle on a fiery liquid. Alf in turn, operates his weapons received from the heavens. How the warheads turn into chants! Meanwhile Emma's son, Fons excels his father, Alf in dexterity. He is in reality, the main hymn in the chants.

Mighty Hipolit, who can destroy many an elephant rank, his feline jaunt that most men fear; he fills the second and the third priest roles in this sacrifice, absorbed in singing absurd, melodic hymns. Aaron, ever engaged in the quietude of meditation dons the role of overseer in the sacrifice. Deafening are the horns and bugles. Frantic, the men beat the tabors and drums, their voices a vulgar roar that bid the attendees to dine at the grotesque festivities. Arrows stir the nectarine; lances cart the nectarine to the diners. While the swords restore the communion, bowls made of the heads of slain warriors. And, libations to the fire is the leftover fluid mingled with their spilt blood."

"D'thor, hideous is this sacrificial ceremony. Lances and maces provoke the sacrificial fire. Even Ostap's son joins this sickening ritual. Missiles shot from Alf's celestial bow swirl into the ambience. Then the car-warriors shoot their weaponry, lifting the ladles and dispensing the precious nectarine. Oblivious to the gore, the diners grab the nectarine in frenzy. Meanwhile, Velasco offers his support to the priests. The men, then install Rodrigo as the sacrificial victim, while this vast army hastens to occupy the seat of his spouse. When the nocturnal rites begin, with immense fury does Lucif slaughter the helpless victims. Powerful Ansell, who chose life from the sacrificial fire, becomes the sacrifice's price." Novio's face had turned impassive, the fury had subsided. In a calmer voice, he continued, "D'thor, the professed ceremony is anything but real."

12

"For many a harsh word, D'thor, that I have spoken and scorned the sons of Aaron senior, just to gratify Rodrigo, I am repentant. D'thor, when you witness my death in the fateful combat with Alf, then begin the subsequent rites of this sacrifice. When you witness Hipolit lap the blood from Ryu's chest, then ends the nectarine-drinking merriment in this ceremony. When the two princes overthrow Hirolio and Dimas, then you, D'thor, pause the sacrifice for a moment. And, when mighty Hipolit kills Rodrigo; that, D'thor, concludes this gory sacrifice. When the widows of Rodrigo's kin and grandchildren grieve and lament, their grandmother, helpless in their midst, on a battlefield wasted by canines and vultures, then comes the final closure to this ceremony."

"I beseech you, D'thor. Save the warrior class from a foreseen, shameful end. Old and wretched, these women and men are. They gaffe at learning. Spare the mercenary of warriors from these professed miseries. I beseech you. Let them meet their end when their weapons clash on these sacred grounds. They deserve no other death, D'thor, no other. On this sacred ground, D'thor, please fulfill your highest mission. I pray, the degraded warrior order attains the highest abode. As long as men can view the towering hills and swim the mighty rivers on this planet, let men sing the veteran's glory and the wise recite fables about this predestined war. The fame, the men achieve in this battle will be their crowning wealth. D'thor, bring Agata's son, Alf before me in battle. I ask no more. But, promise not to speak a word of this discourse to anyone."

Arsenio, viewing through his celestial scope, spoke incessantly on the happenings to Daniel, his voice trailing to a murmur. Arsenio's heart beat faster as he watches through the celestial eyepiece as D'thor extends his arms and strides towards Novio with a smile.

"Spoken like a true soldier." D'thor paused, "But Novio, does the thought of winning the kingdom not appeal to you? Do you not wish to rule the land given to you by the angels? Whatever you said does not change the fact you are the eldest son of Agata and deserve to be the King of Lakewood."

"You don't understand D'thor, the five princes are not my brothers. They will never be. I may have blood ties, but it ends there. We were never siblings in the true sense, only rivals. Besides, I have no wish to run another kingdom."

Novio spoke in a controlled voice, "I have been searching for answers to many unknowns, now you have confirmed them. I cannot thank you enough. But D'thor, you knew. As a mentor and guide to the five brothers, you knew this. You could have told me of my birth and heritage earlier. It is strange you tell me now."

D'thor ignored the statement, "Now you know who you are, why don't you join the camp of righteousness? It is the right thing; it is the right duty."

14

Novio crossed his arms, "No disrespect, D'thor, but you cannot define my duties. Not now. Not today. I believe I have lived long to recognize well my duties."

D'thor, "I mean no offense, Novio, what then do you consider are your duties?"

Novio, "Foremost, I must protect my friend. He needs me the most."

D'thor waited and added, "And ..." Novio looked away.

D'thor seized the moment. "Even at the cost of setting sail with the dark forces hell-bent on reigning injustice on hundreds of thousands of women and men? Do you once realize your presence in the enemy camp just makes 'team-righteous' fight harder to achieve victory?"

Novio looked away from D'thor, his eyes straying towards the river expanse, "The force has its own reasons, I have mine. Where were you D'thor when their teacher denied me lessons on weaponry because he believed I was not from a royal family? Where was righteousness when all of you refused my participation in the wedding, where my winning the hand of Jada was certain? Where was righteousness when I had to convince every single person how a person of such low birth could even become a king? Righteousness never took my side, D'thor, but, I know one friend who did - Rodrigo."

"And that makes my duties - one-sided."

"Novio, events that happened thirty, perhaps forty years before are in the past. A minute before, you said the past is behind you." D'thor spoke, his voice gentle, persuasive and yet impatient, "Why do you still bear the grudge? I always held you above all that, Novio." D'thor stepped down from the car and looked up, "Why, Novio, why? Why do you choose a path that has no merit? A path only endorsed by Rodrigo, no one else. Be honest, Novio, don't you agree Rodrigo is in the wrong, he is the one responsible for this war?"

Novio hesitated, "Yes, I do."

D'thor, "What then, is your motivation in fighting this war? The five princes have their reasons, Rodrigo has his. What is your purpose? What will you gain from this war? Nothing can reverse the past incidents. Is it just petty vengeance?"

Novio, "In fighting this war, I gain nothing. Like Dimas, I am just another lone warrior in this battle - fighting for nothing. Dimas bound to his vows, is powerless. I am not helpless, I can walk away from the battlegrounds, or fight when I want. But, I won't."

"Desert my friend at an hour he needs me the most? I won't. I know Rodrigo has his scruples. Who doesn't? That does not undermine my gratitude or camaraderie."

16

D'thor, "What if both the parties settle for peace? What if the war never happens? How are you going to re-pay your debt of friendship?"

Novio laughed, tears of joy formed a film on his wind strained eyes, "Apologies for the laughter, D'thor. When the lord is trying to persuade me to change sides, this war is anything but inevitable."

D'thor, "Novio, what if the five-bejeweled princes win and invite you to become the king of Lakewood? Remarry Jada, who you could not win in the wedding contest!"

Novio waved his arms, "No, D'thor, no. That is not even a possibility. At the end of this war, either Alf or I will remain alive. No matter which side wins, only one among the two shall survive this war. As far as it concerns Jada, I know I have insulted her in the most unjust way, I even called her a slut in the court room. I should have never said that. It's so unlike me. Even if she approaches me today, the giant wall of insult I only created, shall stand between us. I am not worthy of her now. There was a time, I was — enamored by her beauty. But no longer. It's too late. Sorry, D'thor, it is way too late."

"Novio, do you realize, victory to the five princes is certain?" D'thor paid no heed to Novio's defensiveness. "The flag-post that carries the Aaron banner flies high, triumphant. It favors Aaron's son, Alf. Miron, the divine artificer reinforced the flag with otherworldly alchemy to confirm it furls high. Other heavenly beings in every form and beauty are sure of this victory. The truth, revived and rejuvenated, radiant as Alf, spreads like wildfire, unobstructed by hills and trees. When Alf appears in the battle, his car drawn by white steeds with the reins in my hands will lug the dreaded, lethal weapons. The mere twang of celestial bow piercing the blue firmament like thunder will wipe out achievements of the glorious three ages. What remains thence, I shall confine to the darkest with Kraal embodied as the present."

"The minute you witness invincible Aaron, devoted to staunch meditation, like the very Sun in all its brilliance, crushing his foes, then all traces of three ages will cease. When you behold in battle the mighty Hipolit dancing, having quaffed Rodrigo's blood, like a fierce elephant, its temples rented, having killed a mighty antagonist, then all signs of three glorious ages will dissolve into the era of the darkest."

"The world shall no longer witness the effulgence of the mighty Sun. All that will cloud the earth will commence at the mercy of the new ruler of darkness."

"When you return to the palace, remind the King, the chieftains, the present month is anything but, delightful. Food, drink and fuel is in abundance. Plants and herbs steeped in strength, grow in vigor. The rains festoon the trees with flowers and fruits. And flies and diseases, there are

18

none. Roads are free from mire; the spring waters taste their best." D'thor stretched his hands. "Feel the weather, it is neither hot nor cold, though the Sun has turned his face away." D'thor looked away at the dolphins, who were no longer engaged in their playtime having receded to the deep. "Seven more days, Novio. Yes, seven. Then arrives the fated day, with the new moon rising, setting in motion the wheels of the great battle. A day presided by war gods."

D'thor paused, his eyes distant, but tense. "Go, tell the kings, Novio, when they come to fight, I will, in all eagerness, fulfill their last wishes. Those kings and princes drawn to the dark forces, misled by Rodrigo, shall earn their death by chosen weapons."

Arsenio engrossed in listening to the conversation through his mystic apparatus, blurted to Daniel, "The last dialog has an inconceivable impact on Novio. Novio, his hands held in submission, kneels before D'thor."

"You, who know everything, why do you beguile me O lord?", Novio whispers, his eyes down, still kneeling. "Yes, I can sense the catastrophic destruction of the earth. Cold-bloodedly, Rodrigo and I have escalated the situation to a point of no return. But this tide fails to return to the sea; the stream of Karma will dash the hopes of any return as fast as the torrent. And, D'thor, when strikes this fierce battle between the five princes and Rodrigo's men, blood will sludge this beautiful land."

19

"Under the wrath of fiery weapons, the god of death will lead the kings and princes commanded by Rodrigo to his abode."

"Frightening is this vision. Terrible portents and commotions will soon consume this picturesque land. These omens make me tremble O lord. My hair stands on its end. Rodrigo's defeat is certain. And so is Aaron's victory. Even the celestial planets emit negative vibrations. A dreadful slaughter of friends and the living shall plague these grounds. Without doubt, D'thor, a dreaded calamity perpetrates the Rodrigo's dynasty. Having lost lunar benevolence, the lunar nodes and the mighty Sun hidden behind the clouds will cross each other's path with viciousness, the world has not witnessed. Whirlwinds, tornados and earthquakes shall appear from nowhere. Elephants will cry in fear, canines will bay, while the steeds, D'thor will shed copious tears, abstaining from food and drink."

"These portents are signs of a terrible calamity. I foresee nothing but a terrible slaughter. The battle elephants, wolves and steeds in the five-brother camp wheel along their right cheerfully. There cannot be a doubt of their success. The same animals, pass by their left in Rodrigo's army, fenced by strange, incorporeal voices that haunt them."

"Signs of an imminent defeat."

20

"So many auspicious birds, peacocks, swans, and even cranes trail the five-brother campers, while vultures, hawks, ghouls, locusts and killer bees, in flight and herds, follow the Rodrigo camp. Drummers in Rodrigo's army beat their instruments, but they yield no sounds, while those at the other camp roll without being struck. Even the water-wells amid Rodrigo's encampment howl in miserable cacophony."

"Defeat. Nothing but defeat."

"D'thor, the heavens pour flesh and blood on Rodrigo's soldiers. From nowhere, mists, fogs, walls, deep trenches and porches appear above our encampment. A dark halo dismantles the Sun's aura. Twilight hours at sunrise and sunset scream of great terror. Hideous cry the jackals."

"Indications of tremendous defeat."

"So many inexplicable birds with just one wing span, with one eye, perched on one leg, hover around Rodrigo's encampment at nightfall. Men scramble for cover on hearing their shrill cries. Never have I witnessed such fierce creatures or such horrors."

"These birds point to a defeat that is imminent."

"It is a shame, the way Rodrigo's soldiers blatantly ridicule the wise, and the learned. If you look around, a mysterious phenomenon bathes the horizon on the east of Rodrigo's encampment in colors of crimson; it fills the south

21

with the hue of fiery weapons. The west casts earthy colors. D'thor, the world around Rodrigo's encampment appears ablaze. Such portents promise many untold dangers. I have seen in a vision, Aaron along with his four brothers access a palace built on a thousand columns. Dressed in white robes and white hats, the five appear seated on white seats. In that vision, you wrap the blood-dyed earth with awful explosions."

"Aaron, with a new burst of energy, ascends a heap of bones merrily sipping buttered porridge from a golden cup. He then swallows the land handed to him by you. Now I know with certainty, he will rule the earth. And then, fierce Hipolit stands on the summit pulverizing this planet. Now I know with certainty, he will slay us all in this fierce battle."

"Yes, victory sides the camp of righteousness."

"Incidentally, in this vision, I perceive Alf armed with his celestial bow and missiles along with you mounted on a white elephant. Such a mesmerizing sight. No one can doubt, O D'thor, that in this battle, you will slay all the kings who Rodrigo has swayed. The young princes from the five-princes group along with mighty car-warrior Julian appear in the scene adorned in white, wearing white bracelets, cuirasses, garlands, and white robes. They climb into such excellent vehicles protected by large canopies. Striking is their white against other kings who appear in red. Then comes the fearsome car-warrior Dimas in a tall vehicle. Daniel's son and I join their procession. We soon reach the

22

cosmic quarter ruled by sage Gervasio. It is now so clear that death god's abode is our immediate destiny. Every king and mercenary consumed by the celestial bow's fire will join us there."

D'thor interrupted Novio, "Novio, earth's destruction is inevitable. But I can suggest a way around it. You can prevent some of the destruction if you accept what I say. In such times, I reckon the heart fails to analyze right from wrong. Realize it Novio, your heart is under such duress."

"But D'thor," Novio remained consumed by his vision, "If we emerge alive from this great battle, then we meet here again. Otherwise, D'thor, we shall meet in the heaven, somewhere. It dawns on me that the latter is the only possibility left for me." D'thor stared at Novio. 'Was Novio dismissing him?'

"Novio, I do not think it is ever late. If a war is fated, it will happen. I had dismissed your query earlier, which I will answer in brief now - having you on the side of five-bejeweled princes alters the course of this war. I ask you to think again about your decision, but, I will honor your honest choice of alliance for now."

For a moment, D'thor stepped back from the river bank, he shook the garlands from his neck and placed them in the rough, gray waters.

Arsenio, his eyes steady on the scope, spoke to King Daniel, "They return in silence to the palace gates. None exchange another word. The hour is toxic. Novio holds D'thor to his bosom before he descends the car and dives into his carriage." The scope no longer operative, Arsenio steps away, his mind in a whirl. Apt was the time to speak no more and reflect on the foretold happenings. 'What tempted Novio to reject the leading hand of D'thor? Was he cursed to perish in the isles of error?' His eyes strayed to the hallway overlooking the royal gardens. 'Every siphoned layer of darkness is just an antithesis of light. Every one of them concealed in their shadowy depths, the seeds of error. If in the beginning was the word, creation came from its expression. Born was light. Consciousness was light. But, to dismiss consciousness …' Arsenio felt the tremors go through his muscle mass.

He was glad, the biased king did not witness his terror. 'Wait. Where was Herm, the chieftain of the god-warriors? D'thor spoke of Herm's day. Herm, yes. That was their only hope.' He turned to the king; all he saw was the empty throne. 'The light that Herm carries can expose the concealed secrets. And the incandescence exposes Kraal, who hides the truth in the distant canyons. Buried somewhere in those undulating ravines was the answer to this professed battle.' Arsenio's scream went unheard. There was a not a soul in the hallway.

24

The chariot increases speed, the wheels blazing through the soggy alluvial tarmac. 'I hope Arsenio informed the king about this event.' His own voice startles him. On seeing Drake smile, D'thor dismisses all thoughts of Lakewood. The car rolling in high-speed on the empty highway races against the fog closing behind them.

Darkness dances to the rhythm of the car, assuming every form, every silhouette - a swarm of locusts could not have done better.

'Nothing stands in the way of the dark avalanche. Nothing.' D'thor remembered, he had one more task to carry out. 'When lost are brilliant colors to earth's inhabitants, their degraded sight would fail to perceive light in the dark? Time alone knew the answers.'

'Perhaps Kraal did.
Predestined king of darkness.'

***

DARK MOMENTS

Three-wheeled journey opts for a fourth charioteer
Quiet rolls an innocence-phase in the travel cart
But third corrupts the second; wisdom granting war
Only fourth in the dark holds a promise to a fresh start

Just once. Ponder, how you appeared before
Unlike a vernacular tradition, to which you'd never agree
Contrast the old with the new. Not the ages four.
Where fits the dark-spell in this imagery?

Did you just stop to a music never done?
What the eyes didn't see, ears declined to hear
Senses trapped in dusk, where escape there is none
Think. How sound transits the dark, sails into the clear

26

DARKEST

Vision, rationed in dark. Sight, partial to two. Not three.
What two eyes fathom? Why other eye hears carefree?

Gold pebbles in sand, forefathers ascribed their mark
Promoting their forbearers' coded jewels
Knew they, where to look, when turned on was dark
No blindfold, they'd listen in select grammar schools.

'That was then,' cries Arth, 'Why is this minute opaque?
Why is the way out of this mess a lyrical curse?
Why are rays of change for the few so fake?
Why Nis elite are spared, caught snatching a purse?'

Exiled from a golden land - lonesome, betrayed
Arth toiled every ground, tree limb and bark
Racing the hills, his steps, the everglades flayed
Every hour deeper into the realms of the dark

Above him, repeated the overcast gray nimbus
Away from three villages scoured by a geometric arc
Arth, the golden dominion's banished witness
Weak he felt, against the rage of the dark

Away from the village of Nis perched to his left
Arth walked through the town of Favio in detest
Tallest amongst the triad it stood bereft
Walked he from Synta, by far the smallest

Perturbed by thoughts of tribal chiefs that ruled Earth
Old wars. Old blood. Blood smeared in groves of green
Trees with pear trees offer shade. Stops young Arth
Stops to pine for his loss. Tears fall in between

Without her, the spring season is but bland
Dawn stays dark. Days are dark. They harbor little light.
What screams in day with fright is struck at night by the sad
Every code of knowledge turns dark as the night

'Return to Nis? Was there a glimmer of chance?'
Why couldn't his tired mind overcome such fears?
'Eerie is this misery, from dawn until tide advance'
Succumbs he, back to a flood of tears

'What good is this necklace of gold?
Or even this band I wear on my wrist?
How the months pass? How my feet tread the cold?
Nothing settles the uncalm in my chest'

Oblivious to a bank of clouds in place
Point they, to galaxies where live the sages
All his thoughts centers on his love and Nis' river-face
Lit so well, the town, by Sun's many phases.

28

DARKEST

When all else ruddy'd in the shadow of doom
No dark, visible. Dreams he, of every Nis lit room.

Lost in marshland shadows of a distant upland
Hidden by Cha and feathery starlit showers
Nothing 'bout those villages can Arth understand
The little region known for its unique prowess

DEV BHATTACHARYYA

DARKEST

On Arth's weary shoulder, strong Blue flaps
Walls and floors and stairs, they both clamber
'Stop Arth, I ask again. Stop fighting facts'
Blue's voice roars in anger.

"Descendant of Jada, you must decide
Contrast you, with a less favored branch of the family
They, who live in the darkest, with propriety and pride
They call themselves Ar, naturally."

Blue leaves Arth to greet the crescent sky
Seeking a glimpse beyond the dark pretext
Thirty lunar years stopped not his old wings to fly
Sweet was the wind above lowlands of the darkest

When folks gathered in numbers - listen to wise Blue
Spoke Blue like none other, in pockets of slow

DARKEST

"Dark 'twas. In the gloom, buried was a key
Calm were the pods, nothing stirred in the sea
Slumbered everything that was, and would be
Nothing out-of-place - all alone was He."

"But who was He? And, why the missing light?
'I am my energy's quart,' rumbled His voice
'Rest stays hidden in the nectar of dark quiet'
Key to darkness left to his choice"

"Sunken in the dark at his own discretion
Urged a consciousness, breathing within
None but Him, held the key to the expression
Heard he again, the notice, loud in the din"

"Thus, Did He free the expression
He patched a heart that pumped riches of blood
'Blue Jove,' cried the entombed, seeing the crimson
Burst forth stars, distanced they, from the Lord"

"Heavens, he made. He made this earth
Earth had no form. Empty was all quarters
Darkness brooded on the deep that sought birth
Hovered the spirit over the tepid waters."

"Light, He let there be light.
Light was good, light was never dim
For light was day, dark was night
Kraal was just born, why the grim?"

"From His dark, elect He, a song of rhythm and dance
Cosmos swirled in size from this energy
From the good of His foot's romance
Bathed in light, He let darkness run scot-free"

"Deserted darkness, young Kraal reined it in
Dense was the ploy, his own shadow hid him"

"Years went by. Many thousands. Only He knows.
Lights dimmed, while the universe resumed flight
Earth submerged, the oceans rose
Waves and tides took the lands by sheer might"

"Thousands more years, he let them happen
Ocean rose again, fire engulfed every land
Wise, blessed with light and a fiery passion
Moved to neighboring Nis as D'thor had planned"

"With it started the world at war
Kilns, families, horses, elephants and warriors slain.
Harvests parched. Cattle preyed. Terror and gore.
Novio killed. Could Arsenio ever explain?"

"The war, why didn't D'thor avert?
Thought-forms, why did they rotate?
His thoughts, within and without. He let them skirt
With his thoughts he sealed the village Nis's fate"

DARKEST

"His thoughts spun to hearts larger than heads
For the heads offer only the fanciful and vain
Hunger of every heart sewn in his scarves' threads
In the heart, suffering alone could heal the pain"

"In the new world, new rules played
True light narrowed just to the three villages
All else confined to the dark and it's shade
No shred of light visible in Kraal's unlit cages"

"In the dark, eyes and senses suffered no loss
Men still fought, one against the other
Dark region succumbed to another where they'd cross
Women vied to win the men in their darkest attire"

"You wonder, why women and men are so shrunk?
Was it the nectar of darkness, Earth had drunk?"

"As you fly up the stairs of the old castle
From the landings, stare out the windows unseen
Grasp the distant darkness amidst the quiet bustle
Hoping for a shred of light in the green"

"Fly? No need. Every flight is within.
Fly as the swan. From a fiery egg, the swan seized birth
Modeled in the green glen, borders the higher heaven
Life, matter, mind. The head is threefold on earth"

"Buried in the head, eyes are the hymns of old
Wings span the vast, sputter at the edge
Broken limbs dance to every rhythmic fold
Webbed feet clasp the remains of subtle knowledge"

"Why do you groan my friend, why do you cry?
Why do all you people multiply?"

"See here Arth, look at this quick
A circle, I draw with this twig in hand
Same circle you draw from the wisdom of logic
Render it I, through consciousness and mind"

"Such is that little world, I smother with brilliance
Blessed it is by an order you can't imagine
Your world moves by darkness, mine by radiance
You wonder, how does this happen?"

"I see as you do, but I hear what you don't.
His Word, I hear. I feel. I speak them to you.
In the darkest, only the Word is your silver tone.
Glimpse of the bright, I can bring to view."

"Arth, burn those murky jeans, they don't matter
Come to me in all sincerity
Eat nothing. Not a crumb. Don't touch water
Come, I will offer a glimpse of reality"

34

DARKEST

"To think the D'thor dolphins bore no pain?
Or Novio's cats had nine painless lives?
Thoughts so thoughtless in a blue-less brain
You feel pain. No sooner, a gift of painless arrives."

"This church, we kneel on, is self-manifest
Arth, see the floors and walls, they are never imposed
It is the place where lies the celestial nest
Every door, He channels. They are never closed."

"His children will depart the realm of light and dark
While here, today; they endure pain as I do
To appreciate healing, in suffering they embark
Rewarded with the bliss, they go through."

"But, Blue, my home in Nis", Arth cried
"Why can't I ever see it again?
Against some absurd rules in Nis, I once defied
Critical of the bigots, I had gone to complain."

Blue spoke, "You can't see Nis from the dark of silence
No. But, in your ears, you hear it's freedom of radiance."

"Be radiant. Be free
Beguiled is the parade of darkness or light you learn to defy
Don't lose yourself in the rhythm of a dead sea
Bounce the river blue, and blue shall turn the sky"

"Lift your heart, stop being the mortal man
Through the distant wall of silence
Escape the dark, one dark side at a time. That's the plan
Soon you will find the flare of lighted spaces"

BLUE'S NOT DARK

Arth glances at the night. 'It's late summer.
See how the dark clouds rush. And, winds so vile.
Storm strikes the tree. Scurries downhill my lumber.
Why, slashed are the dunes, for many a mile'

"Dead is every flower," Arth's lost his candor
"So dark, Blue. But, you glisten as the chrome
Be tonight's beacon, Blue. No, don't answer.
Send a message to my distant home."

"Easy. Just ride the wings of the sudden breeze.
Smother the fearful doves when they join you in the dark
Not the rebel swan, who will attend your ardent flight
Their play lost in the cloak of your nightly spark"

"Blue, where is my lost love?
Does she clamor for me, does she wonder where I am?
Blue, visit her once. Get on the highway above
Hurry, you must. Before the winds and the snow slam."

"Storm, I don't need your noise
Earth, greet the din. No. Without that grinning green
Think of every child who screams, forsaking toys
They scramble O storm. Dare you make another scene"

Soggy turns the ground - snow breaks through
Crunches the cool and frost under a weak sun
"That doesn't stop you. Pleasant be your flight, Blue
Wish your next voyage brings you a different fun"

"See the farmhands in their faded jeans
They admire your blue haze from their cupped gaze
As they rush to close the season on their machines
To Nis! To Nis! A trail you can surely blaze"

"Nis lies beyond that glorious rainbow
You see it not against the dark mountain tips
Once you are past, new seasons sing. Hues glow.
Every peacock's blush dance to placid scripts"

"Your flock, Blue, they graze the twin hills
Stroking the canvas with debris of snow
Soft heave those mounts caught in dark and chills
Wet is the snow paint on plaid greens of a shy willow"

"Shower in those flakes, if you must
Frolic, you may, in the woods, with laughing maids
Resume your flight, to where ambles the sunburst
Where hides the towns in the mountain shades"

DARKEST

"O Blue, see, how the cloud sheds its flakes
How the frolicking deer's spots turn into white
Did you lose your way? Arrive at a different place?
While your flock sipped the snowy sight"

"No, don't pause, seek you must, my forlorn love
Stop you mustn't, those estates, they entice
Not even at the garden of the peacock and dove
Tarry no more, convey my message in concise"

"As you fly across the fabled city of York
Luxury entices the senses. Why not ask for more?
Sip the sweet water of Hudson. Pause at central park
Echo the city's chuckle, mute its roar."

"Don't you rush to the northern lights
Yield first to the polite towns in the fifty states
Watch when you go past those soaring spikes
Shivering in the snow, they still praise your grace"

"Ahead flows the Delaware steady
Merry is her chatter. Foam dances at her feet
Fishes flock to the navel of her eddy
Stop if you will, rock to her intoxicated beat"

"Brother Blue, there stands the hallowed church
Lit is her path with sparkling wicks everywhere
Close you must be, to the end of your search
Quick, beckon the devout to a prayer"

"Hasten, nimble Blue, here comes the new sun
Closer you are to a destination dear
Feel the swing in power as you leave the rays of none
Wafts a new breeze to kiss away every lotus' tear"

"Tailwinds whip the flight's slow progress
Melted streaks of snow stare from a chimney top
They seek the languor of your wing's caress
Promise them no more than an altitude drop"

"Joy and sorrow caught in life's merry wheel
Some struts relish the up, some face down
Up and down, smile and frown. There lies the deal.
One day, I shall return to the crown"

"Fly back, dear Blue, to our dark spread
Can your breath hold a whiff of her scent?
Like the early dawn, how it showers flowers in red
Your return, I feverishly await."

"But blue, you are back, my eyes didn't blink
Speak with me Blue. Your travel. Tell me more
Is she still mad at me? Does she still blush in pink?
Is she just the same, the one I adore?"

"Heavy you are, Blue with lassitude
Can I get you water, tea, coffee to drink?
How can I ever repay this gratitude?
Blue, help me. I am too scared to think"

DARKEST

"Arth." Yells Blue, "Hasten slow. You must.
I hear your pulse throb from north to west
Your flowing breath fans the combust
Listen to this tale again, satisfy your inquest"

"Arth, in the midst of dark
D'thor built three villages in one region
There, D'thor set to rework
Revive his plan against the dark legion"

"Built was Nis, your home, sturdy and large
Favio remained foreign to all
Tiny Synta made the third converge
Nis bathed its banks where the river was small"

"Everything else cast to the shadow of doom
Dark was invisible, so was light in the gloom"

"Time took flight, but dark stood still
Time's like a cloud, twists from one to another
Brilliance of sun thaws dark, but not time's will
Therein ends their short-lived buffer."

"There is no more Nis there. No land of three
That was then, not today
Your love is your cry; a promise to a key
While you were in a swirl, time completed its play"

"But Blue. I just left Nis. Wasn't it yesterday?
Tell me, how can I believe a word you say?"

41

DEV BHATTACHARYYA

"Nis," Blue smiled, "had its end, my friend
D'thor is gone. Long gone. Soon I will be
Arth of the dark, you shall soon transcend
Dusk will bite dirt. You will be radiant and free"

"As in every home, earthen lamps still burn
Your lord is set to your time, he is near and dear
He burns the light within, to which you will return
Count for Him every bead, and loud shall He hear.

"You know not what any end shall bring
If being radiant is being free,
Then this path will blaze with an offering
Walk down the way of love, like a true devotee."

"Losing a transient love, you gained a timeless one
When fate consumes your life, you dare not swerve
In dying, born into life, separation there is none
Let the dark dance. You, it will one day serve."

"I am the shade of D'thor, if you didn't know
To you; to the crowd, I am his shadowy blue
Destined, you and I'll walk this path, ending in a plateau
We will swathe past this dark mountain of snow"

***

42

RANDOM NOTES

For thousands of years, human representation of Sun remains an icon, a charioteer on a car driven by steeds. A common theme across ages and civilizations. Several civilizations even deified Sun, as Sol, Surya, Savitar, Helios or Shamash. In the latter Roman period, the emperors mandated their citizens in worshipping Sun only. Sun's runner up surprisingly is the Moon, aka Luna, Chandra, Soma, Selene, or Sin. Every creature's individuality portends as a product of solar influence and relates to an abstract world of super-consciousness. Personality comes from Lunar stimulus and is the subconscious part of mortal self. Astrology speaks of the third element, known as the ascendant, which refers to the conscious part. That makes us three times confused in realizing our true-selves, or shying away from such realization.

Then, light, its incandescence; darkness, its beacon; semi-light, its rising component molds every living into one conscious ecosystem.

Furze Morrish, author of 'Bridge Over Dark Gods' and 'Outline of Metaphysics' claims, Moon exerts a pull on 'matter' from its dominance on the dark subconscious world. Sun exerts a pull on the 'spirit', marking its impact on the super-conscious level. Thus the lords of the visible and the dark world sustain an yin-yang balance. Jupiter (Greek Zeus) also known as Jove, brought merriment in the tug-of-war between the luminaries. Among the planets, Venus and Jupiter are warm and moist, and Saturn, in contrast, cold and dry and linked with everything melancholy.

Blue had spoken to Arth, "I reckon I am alone. Alone, I stand. In solitude, I pray. But that's me, alone. When I set my foot on the backyard, I expect a mowed lawn, free of weeds. I expect to see no ivy's and lily's questioning my presence. I expect order, and when I witness chaos, I clean the yard, remove the weeds, and the unwanted ivy's. But, that's just me. Do you see yourself different?"

"Did you wonder why fire and ice don't stay together? Because, only one makes history. Though, fire needs ice to prove its point, ice need fire to show her results, even, the Word makes no sense without silence. It makes zero sense when many Words conflict. The fire and ice disparity, and the light and dark divide are so relevant to our lives, Arth."

44

"Portions of what we call life, extends by a finite time, measured by a watch crafted for that species. Other creatures use the higher, celestial clock to measure how long they can use the wardrobe of their bodies. Then one day it is all over. A stranger comes to town and marvels at who mowed the lawn? Who killed the light? Who left the dark?"

***

AUTHOR

Dev Bhattacharyya like many other authors was indoctrinated into the art of writing. In this book, the author has chosen not to let style rule over content. Dev has written many books and articles. Dev lives with his wife; not far from children, grandchildren in the northeast United States.

www.ingramcontent.com/pod-product-compliance
Lightning Source LLC
Chambersburg PA
CBHW021116020426
42331CB00004B/514